GOOD GRIEF!
GOOD GRAMMAR!

A basic (and short) guide to
standard English

Jerry George

Pembroke Publishers Limited

© 1994 Pembroke Publishers
538 Hood Road
Markham, Ontario L3R 3K9

Canadian Cataloguing in Publication Data

George, Jerry
  Good grief! Good grammar! : a brief (and short) guide to standard English

ISBN 1-55138-020-X

1. English language – Grammar – 1950-
I. Title.

PE1112.G46 1994   425   C94-930005-5

Editor: Evlyn Windross
Design: John Zehethofer
Typesetting: Jay Tee Graphics Ltd.

This book was produced with the generous assistance of the government of Ontario through the Ministry of Culture and Communications.

Printed and bound in Canada by Webcom
9 8 7 6 5 4 3 2

Contents

Introduction

The trouble with English grammar is there seems to be so much of it. Let's face it, not many of us look forward to spending our time with a four or five-hundred-page book with a title like "English Grammar and Usage". Yet we all recognize the importance of using "good grammar" in many situations: to create a favourable impression, to express ourselves clearly, and to improve our marks at school and our opportunities at work.

Good Grief! Good Grammar! is intended to summarize for you some of the main rules of standard written English, so that you can be a more effective writer. There may be times when you will want to refer to a detailed reference for more information. But this book offers you some basic guidelines, including

— clear definitions of the terms we use to talk about English;
— explanations and examples of the major "rules" of English grammar;
— suggestions for using grammar creatively to improve your writing;
— a "trouble-shooting" glossary of the main grammar pitfalls; those that most frequently confuse even the best of writers.

But, before you begin, here are a few points you should know about grammar:

• You already know more about grammar than you think you do.
Grammar is the system that describes how our language works; how it is put together. It's even been described as the science of putting language in its place! It is complex, but if you speak English, you already know more English grammar than you think. For example, you would likely say,

When I see danger, I run.

5

You wouldn't say,

Danger run I see I when.

You already know the way in which words in English are put together into sentences. You learned it when you learned how to talk. What you may not know are the terms we use to describe this system.

• Appropriate language depends on the situation

Languages such as English that are used over wide geographical areas are divided into *dialects*, varieties of language spoken by particular groups of people. Because English is so widely used around the world, it has many varieties or dialects. So the spoken English in London, England, differs from that of Toronto which in turn sounds different from the English spoken by a person in Kingston, Jamaica. There are even different dialects of English within the same country. For example, in one area of this country, you will sometimes hear people say "youse" when they refer to more than one person, as in "Would youse like some more coffee?"

Children learn to speak in the dialect used in their homes and immediate environments, and their dialect is quite appropriate when talking with friends or relatives. However, often, speakers of one dialect will also understand and use the version of English that is known as standard English, and this is the dialect that is used in formal writing. It is important for students to understand the way that standard English works because this is the English that is used in institutions such as schools and universities. It is a version of English that can be understood the world over, regardless of the local dialect that may be spoken in people's homes.

• Written and spoken English are different

Standard English gives us a common language for communicating. When we speak to another English-speaking person face-to-face or on the telephone, we can usually manage to communicate even if we are speaking in different dialects. This is because, if we can see each other, we can see the listener's reactions to what is being said. If he or she looks puzzled or mystified, we can repeat or rephrase what we have been saying. We can use signs and body language. We can pause or raise and lower our voices. We are more limited on the telephone, but we can still repeat and rephrase. When it comes to writing, though, we have to make our message very clear since our reader can't see us, or ask us any questions. Since writers don't always know who their readers will be, they have to follow rules of writing or "conventions" that everyone has agreed to try to follow.

So although we do know the grammar of our own spoken language, because this is a part of being human, we have to learn the conventions or agreed-upon rules of the written versions of English. These include grammar, spelling, and punctuation.

• Grammar changes over time to reflect changes in usage
Languages that have been used for a long time and that have spread over the world undergo changes. New words are added and some "rules" change. Twenty-five years ago "mart" (as in a drug mart) was not an English word, and nobody could have told you what a "nerd" or a "dork" was. The rule that sentences should not end with prepositions has become more flexible over time. When Winston Churchill was admonished for reportedly saying,
"That is an outrage I will not put up with"
he corrected himself by saying,
"That is an outrage up with which I will not put".
His correction pointed out the sometimes awkward consequences of following rules that have become outmoded.

• Professional writers sometimes break the rules of grammar
You may have noticed in your reading, particularly of fiction, that professional writers seem to break grammar rules from time to time. Here is an example in a short excerpt from *Down with Skool* by Geoffrey Willans and Ronald Searle:

How to Avoid History

Noone hav ever found a way of avoiding history it is upon us and around us all. The only thing when you look at the cuning vilaninous faces in our class you wonder if history may not soon be worse than ever.

Do you see the run-on sentence and can you spot the spelling errors? The authors have deliberately written this as it might have been written by a schoolboy who doesn't know the rules. They are trying to create a certain effect. But remember, before *you* break the rules of grammar for effect in your writing, you need to know what they are! This little book is intended to help you understand some of these rules of written standard English, so that you can be a more effective writer.

The Grammatical Elements of English

The smallest elements to consider when looking at English grammar are individual words, sometimes called parts of speech. These combine into phrases and clauses which in turn combine to become sentences. Sentences can be of different types with different functions. The diagram on page 10 shows the various elements that make up English grammar.

Types of Words (Parts of Speech)

Knowing the names for the function of words in sentences is mainly useful to help you discuss your writing. (For example, someone might say to you, "Try to use more adjectives", or, "It would help if you made your verbs more precise"). So use the explanations which follow as references just in case you need them.

The first thing to know is that words become parts of speech only when they are used in sentences. The part of speech they become is determined by their use in the sentence.

Here we go.

Content Words

These carry most of the meaning in a sentence.

Nouns

Nouns are names and identifiers of people, places, things and

A MODEL OF STANDARD ENGLISH GRAMMAR

Types of Words
nouns, pronouns
verbs, verbals
adjectives, adverbs
prepositions, conjunctions

Clauses
have subjects and verbs
can be independent (stand
    alone)
can be dependent (need
    more to complete the
    meaning; can't stand
    alone)

Phrases
no subject or verb
a fragment of a sentence

Sentences

Kinds

Complex
has 1 independent
clause, and 1 or more
dependent clauses

Compound
has 2 or more
independent
clauses

Simple
has 1 subject,
1 verb, and is
independent

Functions
— to make statements (assertive or declarative)
— to ask questions (interrogative)
— to give commands (imperative)
— to express surprise or strong emotion (exclamatory)

ideas. They become nouns when they are used in sentences as doers or receivers of actions:

> The **player** popped her **bubblegum**.
> (Both words in bold type are nouns — one doing the action, the other receiving it.)

> An **adult** is a **person** who has stopped growing at both **ends** but not in the **middle**.
> (Words in bold type are nouns.)

Proper Nouns

The names of specific people, places, companies and institutions are capitalized. They are also known as *proper nouns*.

> **Throckmorton P. Goldersleeve** had a radio program with the **National Broadcasting System** in **New York**. **Martin** visited **Mount Robson** over the **Thanksgiving** holiday.

Singular and Plural Nouns

Nouns can refer to one person, place, thing or idea, in which case they are *singular* (a *desk*, a *box*, the *computer*, a *girl*).

They can refer to more than one; in which case they are *plural* and their endings change to signal this, in most cases by adding the letters 's', or 'es' (the *desks*, some *boxes*, many *computers*, four-teen *girls*).

Nouns are fairly straightforward but watch for two things:
1. *Is it a proper noun needing a capital letter?*
2. *Is it singular or plural?*

Pronouns

Pronouns are words used in place of nouns, often to avoid repeating the nouns.

> *Euphemia loves spinach.* **She** *really likes* **it**.

The pronoun "she" replaces the noun "Euphemia", and the pronoun "it" replaces the noun "spinach".

*A cow is just a machine **that** makes grass fit for **us** to eat.*

The pronoun "that" refers to the noun "machine" and the pronoun "us" replaces the noun "people".

Always make sure your reader knows what noun your pronoun is replacing. Here's an example where it is not clear. We are not sure who the "she" is in the second sentence.

*Sally has a cat. **She** is very beautiful.*

Depending on the meaning intended, this would be better written

Sally, who is very beautiful, has a cat.
or Sally has a cat that is very beautiful.

Pronouns, like the nouns they replace, can be subjects or objects in a sentence. Unlike nouns, some pronouns change their form when they are used as objects.

***Who** was at the party last night?* (**who** is the subject)
*To **whom** were you speaking on the phone?* (**whom** is the object)

Note: "To whom" sounds very formal. In everyday speech you would likely say, "Who were you speaking to on the phone?"

*He wasn't the man **whom** I saw yesterday.* (**whom** is the object)

THE CHANGING FORMS OF PRONOUNS

Pronouns used as objects	**Pronouns used as subjects**
me, him, her, us, them whom, whomever	I, he, she, we, they who, whoever
She gave *me* the money.	*I* gave her the money.
The running shoes belong to *him*.	*He* bought new running shoes.
Please tell *her* about the contest.	*She* heard about the contest.
Don't worry about *us*.	*We* aren't worried.
The teacher sent *them* to the office.	*They* went to the office.

Verbs

Verbs are the action words. They make the sentence go. They allow a sentence to get somewhere. They are the words that tell what the nouns and pronouns are doing, or what is being done to them, or what they are.

> Ahmed **makes** a living as a landscape designer. He **is** very artistic.
>
> **Did** you **hear** the one about the mouse that **went** to Scotland and **became** a moose?

The bad news is there are a lot of rules for verbs. They come in tenses (present, past, future, present perfect, past perfect, and future perfect) and moods (indicative, subjunctive, imperative). The good news is you don't have to know all the rules to be a good writer. If you suspect you might be getting twisted up verbwise, ask for help and trust your ears; listen to your words and see if they sound right.

VERB TENSES		
Present I work I am working	**Past** I worked I was working	**Future** I shall work I shall be working

Present Perfect
I have worked,
 	
I have been
    working
	Past Perfect
	I had worked,
	
	I had been
	    working
		Future Perfect
		I shall have
		    worked
		
		I shall have been
		    working

An important reminder: Be consistent in your use of tenses. When telling a story, for example, don't start off in one tense, then change to another.

X   *When Jamie* **was walking** (past tense) *down the street, he* **meets** (present tense) *Mabel.*

13

✔ When Jamie **was walking** (past tense) *down the street, he* **met** (past tense) *Mabel.*

X *In this short story the hero* **becomes** (present tense) *lost, but then he* **found** (past tense) *his way again.*

✔ *In this short story the hero* **becomes** (present tense) *lost, but then he* **finds** (present tense) *his way again.*

Verbals

Verbals are parts of verbs used in sentences as adjectives (called participles), or nouns (called gerunds). The infinitive form of the verb, formed by adding "to" before the verb, may also function in sentences as other parts of speech, mostly nouns.

A **participle** is part of a verb (often ending in -ed or -ing) used to describe a noun or pronoun.

> *He rushed into the* **burning** *building to get his cigarettes. I saw him* **running** *back out. He had the cigarettes* **clutched** *in his hand.*

A **gerund** is part of a verb used as a noun.

> **Smoking** *is not good for your health.* **Inhaling** *smoke will damage your lungs.*

An **infinitive** is part of a verb formed by putting "to" in front of the verb. It is used as a noun, adverb, or adjective.

> **To smoke** *is not good for your health.* (noun)
> *It is becoming more difficult* **to smoke** *cigarettes indoors.* (adverb)

Because verbals share the characteristics of both verbs and other parts of speech, they can add interest and vigour to your writing.

Adjectives

Adjectives describe or tell you more about nouns and pronouns.

> *Arnold is a* **mean, cranky, unpopular** *man.*

In this example the adjectives (in bold) tell you more about Arnold; maybe more than you want to know.

Except for the odd spelling trap, adjectives are easy. They can help your writing become more interesting and precise.

Adverbs

Adverbs describe verbs or tell you more about verbs or each other. They are used to express time, place, manner, degree and cause.

> *As he walked **slowly** down the dark street, the rain ceased **very suddenly**, and the moon **gradually** appeared in the **quickly** clearing sky.*

In this example the adverbs tell you more about how he walked, how the rain ceased, and how the moon appeared and the sky cleared.

Here's another example, first, with no adverbs:

> *He turned and looked through the window at the leaves falling from the tree.*

Then, with a few adverbs (bold):

> *He turned **slowly** and looked **indifferently** through the window at the leaves falling **softly** from the tree.*

Use adverbs in your writing to add colour and precision to your verbs. Adverbs answer such questions as how, when, where, how often, how long, how much?

Function Words

These act like the glue in a sentence, connecting or joining the content words.

Conjunctions

Conjunctions connect or link words, phrases, or clauses to each other. They are used to help join ideas together.

> *Pat **and** Mike are good friends, **but** that doesn't mean they never quarrel.*

Conjunctions enable you to combine thoughts into longer sentences, and to avoid a series of short, choppy sentences.

COORDINATING CONJUNCTIONS

(connect 2 similar structures: 2 nouns, 2 phrases, 2 clauses)
and, but, or, nor, neither, yet, so, still, for.

SUBORDINATING CONJUNCTIONS

(connect clauses to the main subject and verb)
since, after, until, because, although, if, unless, where, when, while, as.

Clauses that begin with subordinating conjunctions should not be left to stand alone as though they were complete; they depend for their meaning on a main clause:

X   *If there were no gravity.*
✓   *If there were no gravity we would fly away.*
X   *When you take your eyes off your objective.*
✓   *You may start to see obstacles when you take your eyes off your objective.*
X   *Where monsters are kept.*
✓   *Monasteries are places where monsters are kept.*

Prepositions

Prepositions connect or join nouns or pronouns to the rest of the sentence. They show relationships of place (*above, between, in, on, around, through, under, over*), time (*after, during, before,since, on, until*), or manner (*with, like, for, of*). The noun or pronoun that follows a preposition is the object of that preposition.

> *He went **to** the movies; he got out **at** 9:30 and went **into** the restaurant.*

Normally you do not end a sentence with a preposition in writing since its job is to connect a noun or a pronoun with the rest of the sentence.

It isn't necessary to memorize these descriptions of the parts of speech in order to write well. But they can be useful reference points. For example, a reader might suggest that your writing could be improved if you used nouns and adjectives more precisely. (*Car* is more precise than *vehicle*, and *convertible* is more precise than *car*.) So the sentence,

*The **car** was parked on the street.*

can be made more informative by using a more specific noun,

*The **convertible** was parked on the street.*

and this in turn can be made more specific by adding adjectives.

*The **battered old red** convertible was parked on the street*

When you are writing you are trying to convey meaning as completely as possible with only the printed word, and no sound or sight to help. So the more precise or exact the words you use the more likely your reader will get the picture

---

TEST YOURSELF ON THE NAMES OF THE PARTS OF SPEECH

What is the type of word or part of speech of each of the words in bold?:

1. I would like to go ***swimming*** or cycling.
2. ***She*** was very angry and upset.
3. It is easier ***to seek*** forgiveness than to ask permission.
4. You can get cash ***from*** the banking machine.
5. You can't have your cake ***and*** eat it.
6. Oh, what a ***beautiful*** morning!

(*Answers: 1. gerund 2. pronoun 3. infinitive 4. preposition 5. conjunction 6. adjective*)

Sentences, Phrases and Clauses

Parts of speech are grouped into phrases and clauses, which in turn make up sentences.

In this section we look at ways to identify sentences, phrases, and clauses. One of the most common traps that writers fall into is using phrases and clauses as though they were sentences; that is, not giving enough information to the reader to make the meaning clear. In writing it is important to make sure that the reader knows to what or to whom you are referring.

Sentences

A sentence is a group of words that is sufficiently self-contained to independently make sense. A complete sentence has at least one subject and one verb.

Examples:

X   Constantly washed by water.
✔   A peninsula is a neck of land constantly washed by water.
X   You are being inconsistent if
✔   You are being inconsistent if you avoid the sun but go to a tanning salon.
X   To keep flies in the house.
✔   Sometimes screens on windows just help to keep flies in the house.

Functions of sentences

To make statements. *I can't yodel.*
To ask questions. *Do you like yodelling?*
To give commands. *Start to yodel at once!*
To express surprise or emotion. *You don't know how to yodel!*

Forms of sentences

A **simple** sentence has a subject and a verb. The subject is the doer of the action (when the verb is active); it can be thought of as who or what the sentence is about. The verb is the word that tells about the action the subject is doing. Every sentence has at least one subject and one verb.

> ***John sat*** *on the chair.*

John is the subject of the sentence, doing the action; *sat* is the verb which tells what he did.

*The **typist prepared** the report.*

The *typist* is the subject; the verb is *prepared*. Who is doing the preparing? The typist!

A **complex** sentence contains a simple sentence, called an independent clause, and one or more dependent clauses beginning with a subordinating conjunction or relative pronoun.

Spring, which begins March 21, is my favourite season.

The simple sentence or independent clause is *Spring is my favourite season*. The dependent clause beginning with a relative pronoun is *which begins March 21*.

The typist was skilled, but he still made mistakes.

The simple sentence or independent clause is *The typist was skilled*. The dependent clause beginning with a subordinating conjunction is *but he still made mistakes*.

A **compound** sentence has two or more independent clauses joined by a conjunction such as the following: *or, and, but*. Each clause could stand alone as a sentence.

John sat on a chair and drank a cup of tea.
The typist prepared the report, but his boss took all the credit.

Phrases

Phrases are groups of words without verbs.They are clusters of words that are not complete enough to be sentences; that is, they don't have both a subject and a verb. When verbs and other words are added to them, they can become sentences. There are several types of phrases:

Prepositional Phrases

> *to the hockey game*
> *in the backyard*
> *under the chair*
> *behind the cupboard*

These all begin with prepositions and tell you the location of something, but they cannot stand alone. They are incomplete because they don't have anything to which they refer. You don't know what or who is going to the hockey game.

Infinitive Phrases

> *to run away*
> *to jump over a hurdle*
> *to slide into first base*

These are phrases that begin with infinitives. They cannot stand alone because they don't give enough information to make complete sense. Who is going to run away?

> *This is not the first time he has threatened **to run away**.*
> *You have to be in good shape **to jump over a hurdle** like that.*
> *The player decided **to slide into first base**.*

Note: You will sometimes see phrases stand alone in writing. Here's an example:

> *"Where are you going?"*
> *"To the hockey game"*

This makes sense because the answer refers back to the question. The reader understands that the words "I am going" have been left out. So phrases only make sense in a more complete context. They provide information or description but by themselves they are incomplete. In writing, make sure your phrases are connected to the verbs and nouns that complete their meaning.

Clauses

Clauses have both subjects and verbs, and may contain phrases. They can be **independent**, if they can stand alone and make sense. For example,

> *I don't watch T.V.*
> ***I don't watch TV** and **I don't play video games**.*

(Each clause is also a simple sentence. A simple sentence and an independent clause are the same thing.)

They are **dependent**, if they need more information to be complete. For example,

> *I don't watch television programs* **that are violent.**

The meaning of the clause is not clear without the rest of the sentence to which it refers. Here's another example:

> *Gardens in British Columbia are hosts for huge slugs,* **which have big appetites.**

And another:

> *The girls* **who were at the front door** *were selling subscriptions.*

QUICK REVIEW: SENTENCES, PHRASES AND CLAUSES

Sentences have verbs and subjects and can always stand alone. They have four purposes:

1. To make statements
2. To ask questions
3. To give commands
4. To express surprise or emotion

Phrases are groups of related words that can't stand alone as a sentence.

Clauses have verbs and subjects. Independent clauses can stand alone; dependent clauses cannot.

Punctuation

The purpose of punctuation is to allow writers to use signals as substitutes for the sounds, the pauses, and the voice tones they would use if speaking. Proper use of punctuation marks is important if you want your meaning to be clear. One of the things you can do when you are writing and trying to decide what punctuation to use is to read your text aloud.

Here are some examples of some of the most used (and misused) punctuation marks.

The Comma

This is the most frequently used mark within sentences. It is used
1. to separate three or more words in a series or list

> *I like bananas, apples, and pears.*
> *The dreariest winter months are January, February, and March.*

2. to separate two main clauses joined by the conjunctions "and", "but", "for", "or", "nor"

> *I didn't go to the festival last year, and I won't go this year.*
> *Napoleon was a great general, but he still made mistakes.*
> *Will you be going by car, or will you travel by train?*
> *I have never won a lottery, nor am I likely to in future.*

3. to set off an appositive or phrase that explains the noun it follows

> *I was talking about Anne, the doctor.*

4. to separate phrases or dependent clauses that add information, but aren't essential to the meaning

> *He was too young for the war, which took place between 1939-1945.*

5. to set off dates, places, and persons' names

> *He was born on February 21, 1977, in Brampton, Ontario.*
> *You, Katie, are a very understanding person.*

6. whenever needed to avoid possible confusion

> *To win Henrietta, Thomas will have to try to be more*
> *pleasant.*

or

> *To win, Henrietta Thomas will have to try to be more*
> *pleasant.*

Commas have many possible uses within sentences, and the potential for misusing them is correspondingly great. If you are unsure about inserting a comma, try reading your sentence aloud. If a pause seems natural, then use it!

The Colon

The colon is most often used to introduce a list or a long quotation. Note that a colon is only used following a complete sentence.

X *English is spoken in: Norway, Sweden, Denmark and France.*
✔ *English is spoken in the following countries: Norway, Sweden,*
   Denmark and France.
✔ *English is spoken in Norway, Sweden, Denmark and France.*

Joseph Conrad begins his novel by describing his main character: He was an inch, perhaps two, under six feet, powerfully built, and he advanced straight at you with a slight stoop of the shoulders, head forward, and a fixed from-under stare which made you think of a charging bull.

> *(Lord Jim)*

The Semi-colon

This punctuation mark is used when you want to stress a close connection between two independent clauses in a sentence. It is most often used when the second clause begins with one of the following words: *consequently, hence, however, so, yet, further-*

more, otherwise, then, namely, for example, nevertheless, therefore, for instance, that is.

> *I'm sorry I won't be there; otherwise I'd gladly help.*

> *He is a very boring person; for example he talks about himself all the time.*

Quotation Marks

These are used when you are writing the exact words of a speaker, or when you want to isolate a specific word or group of words.

> *The salesperson said, "We have a special deal on this particular item."*

> *The poet W.H. Auden once said, "A professor is one who talks in someone else's sleep."*

> *The word "awful" once meant full of awe.*

The Apostrophe

This punctuation mark is often misused, although the rules for its use are simple.

1. It can indicate possession, in which case add it before the letter "s" if the word does not already end in "s". In most cases this indicates possession by just one person.

> *Lynn's car*
> *life's problems*
> *the judge's decision*
> *the teacher's notes.*

If the word already ends in "s", just add the apostrophe. In most cases, this indicates possession by more than one person.

> *the Browns' house*
> *Charles' book*

An exception to this is the word "its" which does not have an apostrophe to indicate possession. Also do not use an apostrophe with the possessive pronouns *yours, his, hers, theirs, ours.*

2. The apostrophe has a second important function. Use it to replace a letter or letters that have been left out of a word.

> *You're a very clever person. (you are)*
> *It's going to rain. (it is)*

3. Finally, use an apostrophe when writing the plurals of numerals and letters.

> *How many s's are in Mississippi? How many 6's in 36?*

Parentheses and Dashes

Like commas, parentheses and dashes are used to mark pauses in sentences. Parentheses allow you to add information some people may not know.

> *Michael J. Fox (the Canadian actor) is making a new movie.*
> *My cousin (the younger one) is visiting this weekend.*

Use the dash for sudden or abrupt interruptions.

> *If you want to make friends, you should often — even always — be pleasant.*
> *That was an odd — no, a really stupid — thing to do.*

Ellipses

Ellipses are used in quotations to show where words have been left out. For example, here is a statement you might wish to shorten:

> *William Shakespeare, who lived in the sixteenth century, wrote many plays for the theatre, including comedies, tragedies, and histories.*

Use ellipses to show where words have been left out.

> *William Shakespeare ... wrote ... comedies, tragedies, and histories.*

QUICK REVIEW: PUNCTUATION

Basically, you use the following punctuation marks:

a **period** (.) at the end of a sentence to signal a full stop

a **comma** (,) to indicate a shorter pause

a **colon** (:) at the beginning of a list introduced by a complete sentence.

a **semi-colon** (;) instead of a period between closely related sentences

a **question mark** (?) after a question

an **exclamation mark** (!) to express surprise or emotion

quotation marks ('' '') to signal exact words spoken

apostrophe (') for possession or in place of letters left out of a word

parentheses ( ) to add information some readers may need

ellipses (...) to show where words have been left out of a quotation

a **dash** (—) as an alternative to a comma, to express emphasis

Using Grammar to Improve Your Writing

Good writing isn't just a matter of avoiding mistakes. There are many positive steps you can take to make your writing more vigorous, interesting and appealing. You want to be sure your ideas are communicated as effectively as possible, and this is where skill in using appropriate grammatical structures will be helpful.

Revision: Communicating the Content Effectively

When you begin to write, the most important thing is to get your thoughts down, even in point form. You don't need to worry too much at this stage about grammar or spelling. Much of what you write, though, you may have to revise and edit before anyone else reads it.

What's the difference between revising and editing? Revision is the process of "seeing again", and reworking to improve the clarity of your ideas. Only you can revise your writing because only you know what you are trying to express. There are basically four things you can do when you want to make certain you are communicating your content effectively. In light of your intentions and your reader's needs you can

1. **add**
2. **take away**
3. **re-order, or**
4. **substitute/change**

a word, a phrase, a sentence, a paragraph, or a whole section.

The following passage could be changed in a variety of ways:

> As soon as the snow melts, many people like to spend more time outdoors. They might be gardeners, anxious to begin working in the soil. Perhaps, on the other hand, they enjoy cycling and with milder weather they can pursue this outdoor pastime.

1. You could **add** words.

> As soon as the snow melts, many **active** people like to spend much more time **in the great** outdoors. They might be **avid** gardeners, anxious to begin working in the soil. Perhaps, on the other hand, they enjoy cycling and with **the newly arrived** milder weather they can pursue this **envigorating** outdoor pastime.

2. You could take **away words** and phrases.

> As soon as the snow melts,...people ... spend more time outdoors. They might be gardeners, anxious to begin working. ... Perhaps ... they enjoy cycling and ... can pursue this ... pastime.

3. You could **re-order** the passage.

> Many people like to spend more time outdoors as soon as the snow melts. They might enjoy cycling, and with milder weather, they can pursue this outdoor pastime. On the other hand, they might be gardeners, anxious to begin working in the soil.

4. You could **substitute/change** words or phrases.

> When the snow is gone, most people like to spend more time outside. They might enjoy playing baseball or softball. On the other hand, they might be golfers, anxious to get out on the course.

Tips for Composing and Revising

1. Consider your audience.

Unless you are writing quite informally, as in a personal letter, you will want to consider writing more than one draft. If so, your first draft and what it looks like is your business; it can even be in note form. But once you write for an outside audience, you will have to make decisions about the style to adopt. Who will read your writing—a friend, your teacher, a seven-year old, someone living in another country, your girl friend's father, your boy friend's mother, a prospective employer? Try to imagine your reader(s) and adjust your writing accordingly. Should your style be formal or informal?

2. Avoid "over-writing".

Always try to eliminate unnecessary words. This will help you be more precise, and will make your writing more direct and easier to read. For example,

> *In order to understand this idea, it is necessary to be constantly working and studying.*

This could be shortened to

> *Studying will help you understand this idea.*

3. Use the active rather than the passive voice.

The verb is in the active voice when the subject does the action.

> *I **type** my own letters.* (active)
> *Henrietta **drove** her car to the garage.* (active)
> *The artist **painted** a beautiful picture.* (active)

The verb is in the passive voice when the subject receives the action.

> *My letters **are typed** by me.* (passive)
> *Her car **was driven** by Henrietta to the garage.* (passive)
> *A beautiful picture **was painted** by the artist.* (passive)

The active voice is more direct and doesn't take as many words as the passive. Generally speaking, you should have the subjects of your sentences *do* rather than *receive* actions.

> *Phyllis **was given** a new car by her father for her graduation*

could be changed to

> *Phyllis' father **gave** her a new car for her graduation.*

Similarly, avoid overuse of the verb "to be", using strong verbs to improve your prose. When the verb "to be" is followed by a noun that also has a verb form, generally speaking you should use that verb form rather than "to be" with a noun. Here are some examples:

Noun	Verb
drinker	drink
painter	paint
farmer	farm

> *He is a frequent **drinker** of milk*

could be changed to

> *He frequently **drinks** milk.*

> *Claude Monet was a landscape **painter***

could be changed to

> *Claude Monet **painted** landscapes.*

> *In the Middle Ages peasants were **farmers** for the nobility*

could be changed to

> *In the Middle Ages peasants **farmed** for the nobility.*

4. Use parallel structure.

In a series or list, you should begin each item in the list with the same part of speech.

If your list is nouns, use only nouns. For example,

✔ *For this exercise you will need **paper, pencil, pen,** and **an eraser**.*

X *For this exercise you will need **paper, pencil, pen,** and **to erase**.*

If your list is gerunds, use only gerunds. For example,

✔ *I like **swimming, sailing and cycling**.*

X *I like **swimming, sailing,** and **to cycle**.*

In the following list, all the items begin with the same part of speech the infinitive form of the verb.

> *Some of the purposes of writing are:*
> — *to allow us to communicate with others*
> — *to help us clarify what we know about a topic*
> — *to let us use our imaginations.*

not

> *Some of the purposes of writing are*
> — *to allow us to communicate with others*
> — *helping us to clarify what we know about a topic*
> — *to let us use our imagination*

5. Combine short sentences.

Use sentence-combining when you have a series of short, choppy sentences. Try reading aloud to hear if your writing has too many full stops or periods.

> *Bill has skis. They are new. They have the latest bindings.*

These three short sentences could be combined.

> *Bill has new skis with the latest bindings.*

Here's another:

> *Ahmed works everyday at the restaurant.*
> *He works after school.*

These two sentences could be combined to read

> *Ahmed works at the restaurant every day after school.*

Sometimes two independent clauses can be combined by making one of them subordinate.

> *The meeting was postponed.*
> *The subject of the meeting was procrastination.*

Combined:

The meeting, **which was on procrastination**, *was postponed.*

These same two clauses could be combined by changing one of them to a phrase.

> *The meeting* **about procrastination** *was postponed.*

Ideas expressed in clauses or phrases can often be written as single words. For example,

> *The person who is brilliant will surely succeed.*

can be expressed

> *The brilliant person will surely succeed.*

And

> *The house constructed of brick was situated on a hillside.*

can become

> *The brick house was situated on a hillside.*

Writers can become more aware of the effects of sentence-combining if they spend a little time on de-combining sentences. This involves reducing longer sentences to shorter ones, sometimes reconstructing them in alternate ways for different effects.

For example, here is a sentence with several combined ideas:

> *The fog rolled in from the inlet on a vast front, enveloping first the shore line and then, one after another, all the houses on the hill.*

It could be de-combined as follows:

> *The fog rolled in.*
> *It came from the inlet.*
> *It came on a vast front.*

34

It enveloped the shore line first.
It enveloped all the houses.
It enveloped them one after another.
The houses were on the hill.

These single ideas could be re-combined in a different way.

All the hillside houses were enveloped one after another
by the fog rolling in on a vast front from the inlet.

To appreciate a writer's style and to get a sense of how words and phrases can be manipulated for different effects, you might now and then select a passage from a text and "play" with it. You could de-combine the passage, then experiment with re-combining by using adjectives, adverbs, phrases and clauses.

6. Organize paragraphs.

There are few precise rules for paragraphing. Generally, sentences that deal with the same topic are put into one paragraph. When you change topics, start a new paragraph. Sometimes you can use connecting words or phrases to signal a new paragraph (*secondly, on the other hand, alternatively, additionally,* etc.)

Paragraphs usually have one sentence, called the topic sentence, that tells what the paragraph is about. The topic sentence is supported by other sentences that give more details or examples. The topic sentence most often occurs at the beginning, and sometimes at the end of the paragraph.

If you are writing dialogue, change paragraphs every time the speaker changes, even if the speaker says only one word and the paragraph is very short.

"Are you planning to take any holidays?" asked Bill.
"Yes," replied Matt.

Although paragraphs can be written in block form, with no indentation, it is often useful to indent to signal to your reader that you are changing topic. The next paragraph is indented to show you what this looks like.

Try organizing your writing under headings. Ask what
one or two words would give the main idea of what this

part is about. These headings will allow you to "chunk" your writing into paragraphs, and will give you a start for writing topic sentences.

Traditionally students have been asked to write a "three paragraph" essay or a "five paragraph" essay, because this was seen to be a logical organizing principle:

> one introductory paragraph
> one or three middle paragraphs
> one concluding paragraph.

Given the range of possibilities in topics you can write about and the variety of ways of organizing paragraphs, this is often a very constraining format. *As a general rule, do not arbitrarily decide to write a specific number of paragraphs. The number of paragraphs should be determined by the nature and scope of the topic, as well as the style you adopt.*

7. Organize your information.

There are two major kinds of writing you are often required to do. The first is narrative or story, which is made up in much the same way as anecdotes, short stories, and novels. The second type of writing is called exposition. You use this type of writing when you have to organize and present information or explain something.

Richard Saul Wurman in his book *Information Anxiety* points out that there are 5 ways of organizing information: category, time, location, alphabet, and continuum. When you write exposition, explanation, or information, try using one or more of these frameworks.

For example, suppose you have been given or have decided on a very broad topic such as "sports". Where can you begin?

a. organizing by category

What categories could you divide the broad topic of "sports" into? You could use contrasting categories such as the following:

> individual vs. team sports
> professional vs. amateur sports

indoor vs. outdoor sports

sports requiring little or no equipment vs. sports needing much equipment

spectator sports vs. participatory sports

Then for each of these contrasting categories you would list examples. These examples would in turn give you an outline for your essay, and topics for your paragraphs.

b. organizing by time

Using this method, you might discuss the earliest sports, then lead up to popular modern sports.

— What kinds of sports were played in the ancient world? by the Greeks? the Romans? Africans? Chinese?

— What sports were popular in the Middle Ages? Where?

— What are currently popular sports? Where?

c. organizing on a continuum

— from most physically demanding to least demanding
— from most expensive to least expensive
— from most to least dangerous.

Some of these categories can overlap, but choosing one does give you a pattern you can follow as you write, and this in turn helps you to paragraph appropriately.

How easy would it be for you to write on these topics, using one of the organizational patterns? Try it and see!

shoes
trees
hats
board games
cars
transportation

8. Consider using figurative language

Depending on their purpose, writers often use imagery or figurative language to convey their meanings more fully. Consider the following:

- *imagery:* Images, or mental pictures of color and sound help to set the mood of a piece of writing. For example, words such as "darkness", "gloom" and "shadows" create one kind of mood; words such as "sunny", "bright", or "chirping" create a more cheery scene.

- *similes and metaphors:* Writers often use comparisons called metaphors or similes. Metaphors are comparisons of two unlike things that have one or more things in common. For example,

> *Murdoch is a fox* (meaning he has some of the characteristics of a fox).
> *That car is a rocket.*

Similes are comparisons that use the word "like".

> *He looks like a walking pear.*

Both similes and metaphors are so much a part of everyday language that they can quickly become clichès. For example, the following phrases likely sound very familiar:

> *bright as a button*
> *quick as a wink*
> *bold as brass*

Good writers try to avoid cliches and find fresh comparisons to get their ideas across. How could you change the above over-used comparisons?

> *bright as (a butterfly? a good idea? a ray of hope?)*
> *quick as (a bill collector?)*
> *bold as (a billionaire? a blue jay?)*

- *symbols:* In literature, symbols are concrete objects that represent or stand for something else, often an idea or feeling. For example, a snake has been used to represent evil, a dove often stands for peace, a red rose for love.

- *personification:* This is another type of comparison, in which the writer gives human characteristics to non-human things or ideas. For example,

> The sun *smiled brightly*.
> The clouds *glowered* menacingly.
> The wind *sang* softly ...

- *alliteration:* This device, often used in poetry, makes language appeal to our ears. Consonant or vowel sounds are repeated in successive words. For example,

> Slowly, silently the snake skulked ...

Whether or not you try some of the above techniques will depend on your purpose and audience for writing. They might not be appropriate in a business letter, for example, or an information report. However, you might want to try them in more imaginative or creative writing.

CHECKLIST FOR REVISION

Before editing for grammar, punctuation, and spelling, you should have another look at your writing to see if you can improve it to get your ideas across better. Sometimes it is helpful to do this with a partner, who can help you look at your writing with "fresh eyes."

Consider the following points as you revise:

                                                                 Yes   *No*

1. Can you eliminate any unnecessary words, phrases, or sentences?
2. Should you add some words, phrases, or sentences to make your meaning really clear?
3. Should you change the order of any of the ideas?
4. Should you use a thesaurus or a dictionary to find better words to express something?
5. Have you used the active voice?
6. Can you combine any sentences into longer sentences?
7. Is your style appropriate for your audience?
8. Have you checked for any violations of parallel structure?
9. Would comparisons make your writing more interesting or effective?
10. Is there anything else you can do to improve your writing style?

Avoiding Common Grammar Traps

Once you have revised your writing for content and organization, you should edit. This process involves checking grammar, punctuation and spelling by reference to conventions. Following are some of the most common problems with grammar that writers have.

Subject-Verb Agreement

Rule: Nouns and verbs must agree in number.

What's wrong with these sentences?:

> *He go to the back yard.*
> *They loves to eat.*
> *Cats doesn't like water.*

You probably noticed that they don't sound right. The reason they don't sound right is that the subjects do not agree in number with their verbs.

He is singular and requires a singular form of the verb, *goes.*
They is plural and requires a plural form of the verb, *love.*
Cats is also plural, and requires a plural form of the verb, *don't.*

It is trickier to notice subject-verb disagreement when a group of words comes between the subject and the verb, as in

> *The hen with all her little chickens cross the road.*

This should be

> *The hen with all her little chickens **crosses** the road.*

The rule is to find the subject or doer of the action, and make it agree in number with the verb.

Here are a few more rules for subject-verb agreement:

1. When you use there with the verb to be use the singular form ("is" or "was") when the noun following is singular.

> *There **is** a fly in my soup.*
> *There **was** one **person** who didn't arrive on time.*

Use the plural form ("are" or "were") when the noun following is plural:

> *There **are** more **ways** to do this than I realized.*
> *There **were** a hundred and one **dalmatians**.*

2. Generally, use a plural verb with two subjects joined by "and".

> *Lee and Jeff **are** friends.*

When you connect two subjects using "both" and "and", the verb is plural:

> *Both Lee and Jeff **were** at the game.*

(Exceptions are "bacon and eggs", "rock and roll", and similar expressions that are considered to be singular because they refer to one concept.)

3. Use a singular verb with singular pronoun subjects such as the following:

everybody, somebody, nobody, no one, anyone, either, neither

✔ ***Nobody wants** the job.*
X ***Nobody want** the job.*
✔ ***Neither** of these movies **is** playing at the Rialto.*
X ***Neither** of these movies **are** playing at the Rialto.*

Pronoun Forms

1. A pronoun must agree with its antecedent in number. (An antecedent is the word that the pronoun stands for or refers to.)

> ***Miru** raised **her** voice.*
> *The **people** cheered **their** hero.*

In the above sentences, the singular pronoun "her" agrees with its singular antecedent "Miru". The plural pronoun "their" agrees with its plural antecedent.

The following words are singular, and generally should be followed by another singular pronoun form: *everybody, somebody, nobody, someone, everyone, no one, anyone, either, neither.*

> **Neither** *of the girls* **has** *her lunch.*
> **Everyone** *expressed* **his or her** *opinion.*

However, when they are speaking informally, people often use the plural pronoun form. For example,

> *Everyone likes to have* **their** *own way.*
> *Someone broke into the house and* **they** *stole a TV set.*

Some authorities now suggest that when you are making a general statement, and you do not know the sex of the person, you can use "their" or "they" to avoid the awkward use of "his" and "her".

> ✔ **Nobody** *goes to a symphony concert unless* **he or she** *has a bad cough.*
> ✔ **Nobody** *goes to a symphony concert unless* **they** *have a bad cough.*
> ✔ **Everyone** *who crosses a street takes* **his or her** *life in* **his or her** *hands.*
> ✔ **Everyone** *who crosses a street takes* **their** *life in* **their** *hands.*

This is an example of a rule of grammar that is changing with common usage.

2. Most pronouns change form depending on whether they are subjects or objects in the sentence.

Here are some examples that often cause problems for writers:

> ✔ *To* **whom** *were you speaking.* (**whom** is the object of the preposition **to**)
> X *To* **who** *were you speaking? or Who were you speaking to?*
> ✔ *I'll give it to* **whomever** *you like.* (**whomever** is the object of **to**)
> X *I'll give it to* **whoever** *you like.*
> ✔ *Try to find out* **whoever** *is responsible.* (**whoever** is the subject of **is**)
> X *Try to find out* **whomever** *is responsible.*

Remember that variations in usage are generally considered inappropriate in more formal **written** English, although they are quite common in spoken English.

Be careful to use the correct pronoun form in compound subjects and objects.

✔ *They invited Kim and **me** to the party.* (object)
X *They invited Kim and **I** to the party.*
✔ *Between you and **me**, I thought the movie was dull.* (object)
X *Between you and **I**, I thought the party was dull.*

One way to avoid confusion and test whether what you are writing sounds right, is to leave out the first part of the compound object. You wouldn't say,

They invited ... I to the party.

3. When using pronouns always make sure the reader will know to whom the pronoun is referring.

> *Henry told his best friend that **he** would have no difficulty.*

Does "he" refer to Henry or to Henry's friend? Better to reword this sentence so that there is no possibility of misunderstanding. You could rewrite it like this:

> *Henry told his best friend,"I will have no difficulty."*

or,

> *Henry told his best friend, "You will have no difficulty."*

or even,

> *Henry told his best friend that he, Henry, would have no difficulty.*

Here's another example of a confused reference:

> *I finally finished that book on the American Civil War, **which** was very long.*

Was it a long war or a long book (or both)?
How would you resolve this? You could write

I finally finished that long book on the American Civil War.

When in doubt, reword the sentence.

The Comma Splice and the Run-on Sentence

A **comma splice** occurs when a writer uses a comma instead of a period or semi-colon to separate two sentences.

All the schools were closed, there was a big snowstorm.

This error can be corrected as follows:

All the schools were closed. There was a big snowstorm.

or,

All the schools were closed; there was a big snowstorm.

or even,

All the schools were closed because there was a big snowstorm.

A **run-on sentence** occurs when the writer forgets to use necessary punctuation between clauses or sentences. This may result in ambiguity or just plain nonsense!

All the schools were closed there was a big snowstorm. King Charles walked and talked half an hour after his head was cut off.

The best way to spot these errors is to read your sentences aloud exactly as you have written them, or have a friend read them aloud as you listen. Do they make sense? Are they clear? If you have any doubts then think again. What is the problem? How can it be resolved?

Sentence Fragments

Sentence fragments are actually phrases or clauses trying to pass as sentences. Generally, they are missing a subject or a verb. Fragments can usually be recognized by isolating them from the rest of your text to see if they can stand alone and make sense. We often speak in sentence fragments, because our listeners have more context to help get the meaning. When we write, however, we must supply all the context. Here are some examples of sentence fragments:

> *the snarling dog*
> *all the time*
> *flying through the air*
> *which was no more than I expected.*

Each of these lacks a context and is incomplete because either a subject or a verb is missing. You must supply more information, either by putting each in a sentence or by giving each a context so that the meaning is clear. The first one, for instance, could be changed to

> *I was very much afraid of the snarling dog.*

or even,

> *What was I afraid of? The snarling dog.*

Misplaced Modifiers

Modifiers are words, phrases or clauses that change or qualify the meaning of other words. They should be placed beside the words they are meant to modify, or confusion may result. Consider the following:

> *The salesman gave the new sweatshirt to the customer **with the designer logo**.*

(Is the designer logo on the customer's forehead?)

> ***Flying over the city** the airport came in view.*

(Do airports really fly?)

> ***At forty years of age** their first baby was born.*

(This new baby started life late.)

Unless you're trying for humour, make sure you place your modifiers appropriately, rewording sentences when necessary to make the meaning clear. Here's how you could rearrange the three sentences so that the modifiers are placed more appropriately:

*The salesman gave the customer the new sweatshirt **with the designer logo**.*
__When we were flying over the city__, the airport came in view.
*Their first baby was born **when they were forty years of age**.*

Comparative and Superlative (adjectives and adverbs)

When two people or things are compared you use the **comparative** form.

*Mabel is **brighter** than I am in the morning.*
*The sun is **hotter** than any planet.*
*The game was **more** hotly contested than we expected.*

The comparative of short words is formed by adding *er* to the word. The comparative form of longer adjectives or adverbs is formed by adding the word "more" before the word.

*This route is **more** interesting than the other.*
*Bears are **more** dangerous when they have cubs.*
*Deer can run **more** quickly than humans.*

The **superlative** form is used when *three* or more people or things are compared. It is formed by adding *est* to shorter words, or putting *most* before longer words.

*He is the **slowest** person in the class.*
*She won the race because she was **most quickly** off the mark.*

When errors are made it is often because the superlative is used when there are only two things or people being compared. For example,

X *Morgan is the best of the two brothers at singing.*

should be corrected to read

✔ *Morgan is the better of the two brothers at singing.*

Since the superlative is used as the highest degree of comparison it should not be qualified by words like "most" or "very".

47

For example, in the sentence

> *Brian has very unique qualifications.*

the word "unique" means at the top, completely individual; the word "very" should not be added. The words "very" or "most" should not be added to any words that are already in the superlative, such as the following:

> *best, worst, farthest, brightest, highest.*

Redundancy or Unnecessary Repetition

Sometimes writers qualify words unnecessarily. For example, you may have seen the expression "free gift" used in advertisements. A "gift" means something that is free. The term doesn't need to be qualified by repeating the word free. If it's not free, it's not a gift!

Here's another example:

> *They decided to pay their taxes in **annual yearly** installments.*

The word "annual" already means yearly, and so both terms are not needed.

Look again at the heading for this section. What do you notice?

Confusing Homophones

Homophones are words that sound the same, but have different meanings. Some of these are high frequency words, and their different meanings should be kept in mind. For example,

> *their, they're and there.*

The first one, *their*, is a possessive adjective and should be used to modify nouns or pronouns.

> *They admitted that it was **their** own fault.*
> *They put on **their** uniforms to go to the ceremony.*

The second one, *they're*, is the short form for they are.

> *I think **they're** the best people to do the job.*
> ***They're** coming over around nine.*

The third one, *there*, is an adverb of place.

> *Put it over **there**, please.*
> *It was **there** the last time I looked.*

Double Negatives

Do not use more than one negative word to express a negative thought. For example, there are two negative words (n't, and no) in.

> *He **hasn't** got **no** money*

Instead, write either.

> *He **hasn't** any money.*

or

> *He **has no** money.*

Here are some more examples of double negatives; all of them can be fixed by dropping one of the negatives and keeping the other:

> *Alfred **didn't** do **nothing**.*
> *We **weren't** going **nowhere**.*
> **Nobody** is **not** coming with us.*

CHECKLIST FOR EDITING GRAMMAR

After you have revised your writing, you should edit it for possible grammatical errors. It is sometimes very helpful to share the editing with a peer. He or she can read it aloud as you listen, and then you can both discuss ways to improve or clarify the writing.

Grammatical Point   Yes   No   Not Sure

1. Do my subjects agree in number with their verbs?
2. Are the pronoun antecedents clear?
3. Are there any comma splices or run-on sentences?
4. Are there any sentence fragments?
5. Are the modifiers placed correctly?
6. Are the comparatives and superlatives used correctly?
7. Are there any redundant expressions?
8. Are there any confused homophones?
9. Are there any other grammatical points you are uncertain about?

Questions and Additional Comments:

Edited by (self) _____ *(peer)* _____
                    (Name)   (Name)

Date:

Tips on Spelling

There is scarcely anyone who does not hesitate, at one time or another, over the spelling of a word. Yet most of us spell correctly most of the time. The words that give trouble are relatively few in number. In fact, here is a list of the 25 most frequently misspelled words:

again	didn't	know	something	upon
another	friend	let's	that's	went
beautiful	heard	off	their	were
because	into	our	there	when
caught	it's	said	they	where

These are high usage words and give trouble for a number of reasons. One may be that some of them are homophones. They sound the same as other words (their, there, they're; where, we're). Here's a little poem that shows how far you can go wrong because of English homophones. It's also a warning not to trust your computer's spelling checker too far! Try reading it aloud.

Know More Miss Steaks

I have a spelling checker
It came with my PC
It planely marks for my revue
Mistakes I cannot sea.
I've run this poem threw it
I'm sure your please to no.
It's letter perfect in its weigh
My checker tolled me sew.

(Stephen Hume, *The Vancouver Sun*, 21/06/93)

Four of the 25 words in the list use the apostrophe to indicate that a letter has been omitted (didn't, let's, that's, it's). The best way to learn to spell these and other words is not to memorize the rules but to memorize the words themselves. Here's how to do it:

> LOOK at the word carefully
> SAY it aloud softly
> WRITE the word
> CHECK to see if what you have written is correct
> REPEAT the procedure if necessary.

More Tips for Spelling Correctly

You may find some of the following tips helpful:

1. Learn to pronounce the words correctly.

Some words create problems because they are often mispronounced:

> February, not Febuary
> Wednesday, not Wensday
> pronunciation, not pronounciation
> accidentally, not accidently
> could've, not could of
> might've, not might of

2. Recognize common spelling patterns.

There are certain spelling patterns some people find helpful to remember:

use i before e except after c
> *deceive, receive, achieve, chief, belief*

and when sounded like a
> *neigh, neighbour, reign, sleigh*

adding prefixes does not change the word's spelling
> *natural*   **un***natural*
> *mobile*   **im***mobile*
> *run*   **over***run*

when a word ends in a vowel, adding suffixes often doesn't change the spelling

hope   hope**ful**

courage   courage**ous**

but when a word ends in a consonant, the consonant is often doubled when adding -ing or -ed

run   run**ning**

drop   drop**ping**

label   label**led**

There are rules and exceptions for suffixes, and it's best just to learn the most frequently used words:

dine, dining not dinning;

sun, sunny not suny;

hope, hoping not hopping

3. Try using a mnemonic device.

Some people like to use what are called mnemonic devices as an aid to memorizing the words they seem to never be able to remember. Here are some examples:

A fri**end** is a fri**end** to the end (to remember that the word "friend" ends with "end");

One cap and two socks (to remember that "necessary" has one "c" and two "s'"s.)

Dessert has two s's, because you always want **two** of them (to remember the difference between "dessert" and "desert")

The vege**table** is on the **table** (to remember that "vegetable" ends in "table.")

Try making up your own for those tricky words that always fool you.

But in the end, the best rule to follow is

Instead of trying to learn the rules and their exceptions, learn to spell the words themselves. Keep a personal list of words you are trying to learn how to spell, and as you master them put them in a special "victory" column. Group the words that seem to fall into the same categories, such

53

as **enough** and **tough**. *(In each the "ough" is spelled the same and sounds the same.)*

Sorting Out Confusing Words

Even the best of writers at times forget how to use some of the words in this list. They are arranged here alphabetically for quick reference.

amount/number
Use *number* for countable items; *amount* for uncountables.

The *number* of bikes . . .
The *amount* of time . . .

accept/except/expect
Accept means to receive or approve. *Except* means excluding. *Expect* means to think likely.

I *accept* your kind offer of a ride home, *except* I won't be able to leave for twenty minutes because I *expect* that I'll have to lock up everywhere.

affect/effect
Affect is a verb, meaning to change. *Effect* is a noun.

He is not *affected* by heights. I, on the other hand feel the *effect* if I am on the first rung of a ladder.

already/all ready
Already means before this time; *all ready* means completely ready.

If everybody is *all ready* we can get going because the rest have gone *already*.

altogether/all together
Altogether means completely. *All together* means as a group.

If we don't forget the words *altogether*, and we manage to start singing at the same time, we should be able to finish *all together*.

among/between
Use *between* two; *among* three or more.

There are twenty-four candies to share *among* four people, which means you and I can have six *between* us.

bear/bare
A *bear* is an animal (noun); *bare* is without cover (adjective).

Don't ever try to tackle a *bear* with your *bare* hands.

berth/birth
A *berth* is a narrow bed on a train or ship; *birth* refers to being born or at the beginning.

I prefer a lower *berth* on the train.
A new *birth* in the family is welcome news.

brake/break
A *brake* is an instrument for slowing or stopping a machine (noun); *break* is to open up or come apart.

Apply your *brakes* carefully on slippery roads. Be careful not to *break* that glass.

can/may
Can indicates ability to; *may* indicates permission.
You *can* enter a licensed establishment when you are under the legal age. You *may* not, however, purchase any alcoholic beverage.

cite/site
Cite means to mention (verb); a *site* is a place or location (noun).

I can *cite* several examples of historical blunders.
This building is on a beautiful *site*.

cloths/clothes
A *cloth* is a piece of fabric; *clothes* are garments for the body.

How many wash *cloths* are in the laundry basket?

She always wears very fashionable *clothes*.

coarse/course
Coarse can mean rough or vulgar; *course* can mean direction or a series of studies.

I find most heavy woollen sweaters too *coarse*.
He said he would enroll in another *course*.
Nature will run its *course*.

desert/dessert
Desert (noun) is land, usually hot and dry. *Desert* (verb) is to leave or abandon. *Dessert* (noun) is eaten after a main course.

The *desert* is hot in daytime but cold at night.
To *desert* from the army in war time is a serious offence.
The *dessert* consisted of berries and ice cream.

different from/different than
Use *different from* to compare two things; *than* only between clauses.

Your opinion is *different from* mine.
That kitten is *different from* the rest.
I like *different* music now *than* I did five years ago.

dissent/descent
Dissent is to differ, to have another opinion. A *descent* goes from a higher to a lower place.

One senator decided to *dissent* from the majority.
The *descent* into the valley was very steep.

etc.
Etc. means and so on. It is always set off by a comma.

I have to clean my room, study, *etc.*

fewer/less
Fewer is used with countable numbers; *less* with "uncountables".

There were *fewer* people at the concert than expected.
It is usually *less* costly to do simple repairs yourself.

formerly/formally

Formerly means previously or at a time before; *formally* means according to the rules.

I was *formerly* employed by that company.
We have never been *formally* introduced.

forth/fourth

Forth means onward or forward; *fourth* is a rank after third.

They went *forth* bravely to do battle.
She was *fourth* in the high jump event.

good/well

Good is used as an adjective; *well* as an adverb.

He was a *good* prospect in the minor leagues.
When he was promoted to the majors, he did *well*.

hopefully

Often used incorrectly to mean "I hope", the precise meaning is "in a hopeful manner."

X   *Hopefully*, the weather will be good for the picnic.
✔   He waited *hopefully* for the letter.

I myself

I myself (or I personally. . .) is redundant. Generally, it's best to use "I" by itself.

X   I myself think . . .
✔   I think . . .

If I was/were

Use *were* after "if" only when discussing an imaginary or hypothetical situation.

I don't know if he *was* there or not.

If I *were* prime minister, things would be different.

irregardless/regardless

The correct form is *regardless*, meaning without care or regard. There is no such word as "irregardless"; however, *irrespective* is a synonym for regardless.

Regardless of the weather, we're going to the lake tomorrow.

its/it's

Its is a possessive pronoun and has no apostrophe. *It's* is a contraction meaning it is.

The cat was asleep in *its* basket.
It's nice to see an animal at rest.

lie/lay

Lie means to recline; *lay* means to place or is used as the past tense of lie.

Why don't you *lie* down?
He *lay* down for a nap yesterday.
Would you *lay* the book on the table, please?

like/as

Like is used to compare two things. In formal writing, it is not substituted for "as if".

He eats *like* a horse.
It looks *as if* it's going to rain tonight.

lose/loose

Lose is to misplace; *loose* is unrestricted or unhindered.

Try not to *lose* money at the race track.
I prefer to wear *loose* shirts.

me/I

Me is used as an object; *I* as a subject.

Just between you and *me, I* prefer to stay home.

moral/morale
Moral is having to do with right or wrong (noun or adjective); *morale* means confidence (noun).

People who want to lead the country should have high *moral* character.
The team's *morale* was low when they lost.

miner/minor
A *miner* (noun) is one who works in a mine; *minor* (adjective) means small or of little importance.

A coal *miner* does not have an easy job.
I have just one *minor* objection
A ten-year-old is considered to be a *minor*.

muscle/mussel
Muscle is the flesh that moves a mammal's body; *mussels* are shellfish like oysters.

It'll take a lot of *muscle* to lift that weight.
Mussels are a nice addition to clam chowder.

pair/pare/pear
Pair means two; to *pare* is to cut or cut back; a *pear* is a kind of fruit.

The *pair* of them looked very pleased.
We will have to *pare* our budget to the bone
In October you can buy *pears* at the fruit store.

past/passed
Past is a noun; *passed* is a verb.

Stop living in the *past* or you will find that many of life's pleasures will have *passed* you by.

peace/piece
Peace is the absence of war or fighting, a *piece* is a part of.

After the war the combatants signed a *peace* treaty.

May I have a *piece* of that pie, please?

personal/personnel
Personal means relating to one's self; *personnel* is a collective noun for employees.

This is a very *personal* matter.
The company treats its *personnel* well.

principal/principle
Principal means first or most important—or a very important person in a school; *principle* is a value or basic truth.

The *principal* of the school was well liked because he was a man of *principle*.

rain/rein/reign
Rain is water falling from the sky (noun); *reign* (verb or noun) is to rule; *rein in* is to restrain (verb).

I prefer *rain* to snow.
The rider had to *rein* in her horse.
The Queen has had a long *reign*.

stationary/stationery
To be *stationary* is to be still; *stationery* is writing paper.

He remained *stationary* at the crosswalk.
You can buy good *stationery* at this bookstore.

strait/straight
A *strait* (noun) is a narrow body of water between two larger ones; *straight* (adjective) is in a direct line.

The *Strait* of Georgia is off the coast of B.C.
After the party they went *straight* home.

that/which
That begins a clause that identifies or gives essential information about the subject.

This is the book *that* I was telling you about.

Which begins a clause that adds additional information. Note that the clause could be left out of the sentence. Since the clause adds additional information, it is set off with a comma.

The book, *which* is on the bestseller list, is sold out.

their/they're/there
Their is a possessive pronoun; *they're* the contraction of they are, and *there* is the opposite of "here".

Many people save *their* money to buy real estate.
They think *they're* well off if they have no debts.
There are others who just can't seem to save anything.

to/too/two
To is a preposition; *too* means also; *two* is a number (2).

It takes *two* to tango. It takes *two* *to* waltz *too*.

waist/waste
Waste is to use up unnecessarily; the *waist* can be found near the middle of the body.

It seems a shame to *waste* such a large *waist* on one person

weather/whether
Weather has to do with climate; *whether* means if it is true or probable that.

The *weather* is very unpredictable at this time of year.
I doubt *whether* we can do anything about it.

wholly/holy
Wholly means completely; *holy* is being good in a religious sense.

I am *wholly* in agreement that Ghandi was a *holy* man.

who/whom
Who is used as a subject; *whom* an object.

The first person *who* loses ten pounds will be the one *whom* we will sincerely congratulate.

whose/who's
Whose is a possessive pronoun; *who's* a contraction.

Whose keys are these? Could they belong to the one *who's* coming back through the door?

would've/would of
The correct form is *would've*; a contraction of would have. Similarly, use *should've, could've*, etc.

your/you're
Your is a possessive pronoun; *you're* a contraction for you are.

Your conscience is what *you're* going to have to listen to.